"Having been bartending for nearly 20 years, I have had many requests for how a guest can recreate a drink at home. I think it is always important to be clear and concise when writing a recipe for a novice. That is where this book is a triumph. It is cleanly designed, and packed with useful information for the home bartender. It is a must-have for aspiring cooks and entertainers alike. Nothing superfluous. No unnecessary gadgetry. All the tools you need, with easy-to-follow recipes. A more enjoyable and approachable book than many that line the shelves."

JOEY DIEDRICK, How to Cook a Wolf

"Liberal Libations is a great addition to any home bar library! With the aim to cultivate conviviality through cocktailing, Liberal Libations gives easy-to-make recipes ranging from classics, to originals, to batched drinks for parties."

DANI DELUNA, Home Bar Girl

"As the unofficial family bartender, I am often called upon to mix drinks for holiday gatherings and backyard barbecues. Lately, I've been experimenting with large format cocktails as a way to free up enough time to actually hang out with my guests. With concise recipes, tidy design, and juicy photos on every spread, Liberal Libations is the perfect party companion."

GEOFFREY SMITH, Graphic designer, photographer, & cocktail enthusiast

"This is an excellent guide for every beginner that has no idea how to set up a home bar or a basic understanding of the bar tools. It is a system, tool kit, and recipe book that will teach you how to make classic sours for one or seasonal favorites in a batch format for large parties. A must have for anyone looking for delicious libation ideas to entertain friends and family for any occasion!"

JERMAINE WHITEHEAD, Imbibe Magazine 2019 People to Watch

Liberal
LIBATIONS

Liberal LIBATIONS

TRANSFORM SINGLE-SERVING COCKTAILS INTO MAKE-AHEAD BATCHES FOR EASY ENTERTAINING

KIM NEWTON ARISPE

Photography by Bobby Arispe

Library of Congress Cataloging in-Publication Data
Names: Newton Arispe, Kim, author. | Bobby Arispe, photographer.
Title: Liberal Libations: Transform Single-Serving Cocktails into Make-Ahead
    Batches for Easy Entertaining / Kim Newton Arispe
Description: Washington : Kim Newton Arispe, [2019] | Includes index.
Identifiers: LCCN 2019914098

Hardcover ISBN 978-1-7333728-0-0
eBook ISBN 978-1-7333728-1-7

Recipes, book design, art direction, and
    food styling by Kim Newton Arispe
Photography by Bobby Arispe
Illustrations by Leah Sacks
Edited by Annie Fanning

First edition November 2019

randomactsofcomfort.com

ACKNOWLEDGMENTS

Thank you to my friends and family who have supported and encouraged me along this journey. Thank you for drinking with me and cheering me on.

Perry and Angela, thank you for pushing me to believe in myself and this book. Big thanks to Perry for the book title!

Big shout out to Scott and Shannon Austin, and Ben Huff for contributing delicious recipes.

To my sister, Leslie, for jump starting my interest in the culinary world with your creativity and dedication to the craft.

Thanks to my editor, Annie, who embraced my love of the oxford comma. I'm happy we got to work together again!

To Leah, thanks for the beautiful glassware illustrations and for your wonderful partnership every day.

To Bobby, my husband, best friend, and partner in this life—thank you for rearranging our apartment living room over and over again to transform it into a makeshift photo studio, and for sacrificing sunny weekends to shoot the beautiful photos for this book (I know you'd rather be riding your bike). Thank you for bringing my vision to life—I couldn't have done this without you.

CONTENTS

INTRODUCTION

I've always enjoyed hosting thoughtfully curated events, but after my annual Kentucky Derby party, I realized I spent the entire time mixing individual Mint Juleps instead of spending quality time with my friends. When the party was over I wondered if everyone had a good time, even while they waited for their drink to arrive. I thought maybe if I prep and mix cocktails in advance, I could ensure guests would have a drink in hand upon arrival, each sip would be consistent, and I could be a more engaged host.

Starting with my self-proclaimed "Proper" Margarita, I tested this batch concept on co-workers, friends, and family. After the initial thumbs up, I branched out with other batch recipes like the Old Fashioned, Mint Julep, and Moscow Mule. As my drinks gained popularity, I became the batch bartender for friends and coworkers when they entertained. Not only did I have fun mixing up new drinks, but now I was able to be in the moment and enjoy the party.

My hope is this book inspires you to create special cocktail connections in your own home. There's a little bit of magic that happens when we share a drink with a friend, an acquaintance, a coworker, or even a stranger. The cocktail is merely the facilitator—our common ground—but the power of sharing a conversation inspires, comforts, and connects us. These connections can move mountains—one small, meaningful moment at a time.

Liberal Libations is written for the cocktail enthusiast and home bartender who wants helpful tips and make-ahead batch recipes for easy entertaining. Recipes use approachable ingredients, easy-to-find spirits, and fresh fruit juices. Whether you're crafting cocktails for one, two, or a crowd, this book outlines everything you need to be a stress-free host and empowers you to spend less time mixing drinks, and more time enjoying each sip and meaningful moment with friends.

Featuring 85 recipes, this essential guide includes classic cocktails, variations on well-known drinks, and playful originals. Chapters are organized by spirit type, including a wine cocktail chapter. Classic favorites like the Old Fashioned (page 44–45), Mojito (page 121), and Proper Margarita (page 24–25) share the pages with my own inventive creations like

Summer Solstice (page 52–53), the bourbon punch featured on the cover, and Picard (page 56–57), an Earl Grey infused cocktail created in honor of the actor, Sir Patrick Stewart and his Star Trek character, Captain Jean-Luc Picard. Recipes teach you how to make a single-serving cocktail and a party-sized batch, using as few ingredients as possible.

Liberal Libations lays out the essential tools and spirits needed to stock your bar and shows you how to create stunning, yet simple garnishes. Batching delicious, bar-quality cocktails isn't quite the same as tossing together some liquor and juice into a nondescript "punch." Combining ingredients into large-format drinks takes slightly more precision. I've removed the frustrating guesswork and confusing math conversions with multiplying recipes, so you can shop with confidence and mix up cocktails with ease.

Batch servings are based on one 750-milliliter bottle of a base spirit, and crowd favorites also include double batch recipes. Every batch indicates its total approximate volume—rounded for convenience—in ounces, cups, and quarts. No more guessing which pitcher or beverage dispenser to reach for.

Throughout the book, you'll find tips to adjust flavors and swap out ingredients to create different cocktail variations. Every cocktail should taste like a balance of booze, bitter,

sour, and sweet. Since everyone experiences these flavors differently, my goal is to empower you to make each recipe your own. Most importantly, I encourage you to have fun, experiment with your favorite spirits. There is no wrong way to go about crafting the cocktails in this book, as long as you like the way it tastes.

It's time to mix up a batch of cocktails and spend time in warm conversation, catching up with friends and family.

The
HOME BAR

STOCKING YOUR BAR

If you're just starting to build out your home bar, use this reference list to guide you when shopping. Seriously, take this book or a photo of this page with you to the store. I used the Smuggler's Cove book to learn about rum and making tiki drinks, and I plopped that book right down in my grocery cart and referenced it over and over to find the rums I needed. With these basic spirits, you'll have what you need to make all the recipes in this book—not including the wine, for which there are suggestions on those recipe pages. You don't have to purchase everything at once, just grab a couple of bottles with every trip, starting with the recipes you like best. I've outlined my favorites below (in order) based on taste, value, and versatility, but this is your bar, so buy what you like and what's easily available at your favorite store or local distillery.

SPIRITS *(One from each category)*

Tequila
El Jimador Blanco
Olmeca Altos Tequila Plata
Sauza Silver

Mezcal
Del Maguey Vida
Bozal Ensamble
Montelobos Joven

Rye Whiskey
Rittenhouse Rye
Old Overholt
Sazerac
Templeton

Bourbon Whiskey
Woodford Reserve
Old Forester
Four Roses
Buffalo Trace

Vodka
Tito's
Ketel One
Prairie Organic
Reyka

Gin
Botanist
Hendrick's
Sipsmith
Aviation

White/Light Rum
Plantation 3 Stars
Caña Brava White
Appleton Estate White
Bacardi Silver
El Dorado 3 Year Cask Aged

Dark/Aged Rum
Appleton Estate
    Reserve Blend
Smith & Cross
Plantation Grande Réserve 5
Doorly's XO
Havana Club 3 Años

Specialty Rum
Plantation Stiggins'
    Fancy Pineapple

Spiced Rum
Trader Vic's
Bayou
Sugar Island
Chairman's Reserve

Brandy
Martell VS Cognac
Pierre Ferrand 1840
Paul Masson VSOP
Hennessy VS

Absinthe *(Start with a small bottle)*
Pernod Absinthe
Versinthe
Absente
St. George Absinthe Verte
Lucid Absinthe Supérieure

LIQUEURS *(Purchase all)*
Ancho Reyes
Aperol
Averna
Campari
Cointreau
Green Chartreuse
Luxardo Maraschino Liqueur
Mr. Black Coffee Liqueur
St~Germain

Sweet Vermouth *(Purchase one)*
Cocchi Rosa
Dolin Rouge
Martini & Rossi

BITTERS *(Purchase all)*
Angostura
Orange
Peychaud's
Lavender
Old Fashioned
Scrappy's Firewater

BAR TOOLS

It's fun to build a collection of fancy bar tools, but when you're starting out, there's no need to go overboard right away. Here are a few essentials that will make your life easier, and will make you look and feel like a pro.

Jigger

The jigger is used to measure ingredients to a ¼ ounce, so look for ones that have measurement lines on the inside. I find the double-sided jigger to be the most useful. The larger side should hold 2 ounces, with a mark for 1 ½ ounces. The smaller side should hold 1 ounce, with marks for ¾ ounce, ½ ounce, and ¼ ounce. There's a few variations in shape and measurement capacity: bell jigger, Japanese-style jigger, stepped jigger, double jigger with handle, and footed measuring cup jigger. Choose the one that fits your personal style and needs.

Boston Shaker

Cocktails that contain citrus juice are shaken to fully incorporate the ingredients. You'll want to choose the version with two metal shakers—one smaller, one larger—that fit inside one another. It will be easier to find the metal shaker tin and glass combo, but you're going to dread pulling these apart after you shake your drink. They stick together like crazy, and with every hard bang on the counter—to try to separate them—you pray the glass won't shatter. You also might be tempted by the very popular Cobbler shaker. This three-piece set includes a tumbler, lid with a built-in strainer, and a cap. Its fancy silhouette looks nice sitting on your bar, but it's not the easiest to work with. The Boston shaker is the most user-friendly, just be sure to close the tins together at an angle, not straight up and down. After you shake your cocktail, hold the shaker in one hand. Using the palm of your other hand, hit just to the side of where the two tins are sealed the tightest, and they should easily pop apart.

Mixing Glass

Cocktails without citrus juice are stirred instead of shaken. While you can technically stir a cocktail in any glass, these are created to make stirring smooth and fast, and the pour spout makes it easy to transfer your cocktail to a glass without spilling a drop.

Bar Spoon

You might think that there's not much difference between your cereal spoon and a bar spoon, but once you try it, you'll understand. Sure, your kitchen spoon will work in a pinch (like if you're camping) but just like the mixing glass, the bar spoon was created to make stirring fast. Most drinks are stirred at least 20 seconds, so you want something that makes this process quick and seamless.

Hawthorne Strainer

You'll use this staple with every drink that is shaken or stirred. It strains out ice and larger pieces of fruit and herbs. The Julep strainer is another beautiful bar tool, but it's not a workhorse like the Hawthorne.

Fine Mesh Strainer

When a recipe calls for a "double strain" this means you use the Hawthorne strainer to hold back the ice, while pouring the cocktail through the fine mesh strainer to remove tiny ice chips, citrus pulp, and pieces of herbs.

Muddler

The muddler is used to smash fruit, herbs, and sugar at the bottom of a glass or shaker tin to release the flavors. These come in metal and silicon, but my favorite is the handcrafted wooden version with a smooth bottom. If it has a spiked bottom, fruit tends to get stuck forever no matter how much you scrub—and who has time for that!?

Y-Peeler

This is a must for peeling citrus rind to use for garnishes. To ensure your peeler is always sharp, keep a separate one just for your bar—don't use it for peeling potatoes and carrots.

Hand-Press Citrus Juicer

Use this tool to get the most juice out of limes, lemons, oranges, and grapefruit. Cut limes and lemons in half, place cut side down in the squeezer. For larger fruit, cut into quarters to fit into squeezer. An electric rotating juicer is also helpful for batches that require large amounts of fresh orange or grapefruit juice.

ICE

When mixing a single cocktail, ice is used to chill, dilute, and balance flavors. You can control the speed of dilution with the size and amount of ice, and method of mixing. The smaller the ice, the faster the drink is diluted. The longer you shake or stir ingredients, the more it gets watered down.

I prefer to serve most of my cocktails with one large ice cube instead of filling the glass with smaller ice. An Old Fashioned should be served with one large ice cube. I also prepare most Margaritas this way because the dilution and flavor I want to achieve has already happened in the shaker. Some drinks, like the Mojito, require crushed or pebble ice to achieve the right balance, and would otherwise taste too boozy.

While it's easy to control dilution when mixing a single drink, it's a bit of a challenge when making a large batch. It would take forever to shake 16 servings, one by one. You might be thinking, "I'll just add ice to the serving container to chill and dilute my cocktail." The problem is, the drink will taste great at the beginning of the party, but after a short time, it will be a watery version of its former self. And, your guests won't get the same drink when they go for seconds.

To avoid this, water is added to most batch recipes in this book to achieve the dilution that ice would normally provide when a cocktail is shaken or stirred. Ice adds about 25 percent to the volume of a single mixed cocktail, so many people say to add 25 percent water when making large format drinks. Most of my recipes call for less than 20 percent of added water to maintain bold flavors, but feel free to add more to fit your taste preference.

GLASSWARE

Photos throughout the book show suggested glassware for each cocktail, but there's no wrong answer when serving up drinks. Have fun, and let each cocktail's personality shine. When building your barware collection, start with glasses you'll use the most. When entertaining, don't feel the need to purchase 20 of the same glass for each batch cocktail. Use what you have on hand by pairing similar size and shape of glassware per cocktail type. This list is a good place to start your collection:

OLD FASHIONED
(OR ROCKS GLASS)

COUPE

COPPER MUG

HIGHBALL

JULEP

NICK & NORA

MARTINI

WINE
(STEM & STEMLESS)

CHAMPAGNE FLUTE

BEVERAGE CONTAINERS

You'll want to collect a variety of serving containers based on the size of batches and how many people you're entertaining.

Batch recipes include the total volume of the finished drink in ounces, cups, and quarts, so you know exactly which size serving container to reach for.

Carafes and pitchers are great for serving small batches, but I like the ease of a beverage dispenser with a spout for large batches. A punch bowl works well for any size batch.

It's recommended that you to strain cocktails with fruit and herbs. This ensures the spout doesn't get clogged. If you aren't going to serve from a dispenser, feel free to leave the pulp.

EXPANDING FLAVORS

Not all ingredients can be equally multiplied when going from a single cocktail to a batch. Simple syrups, liqueurs, and bitters, intensify in larger quantities so each recipe in this book has been carefully adjusted for balance. If you're unsure of a certain ingredient or flavor, start with less than the recipe calls for and gradually add more until the flavor is right for you.

JUICE MEASUREMENTS

Fresh-squeezed juice is a must. Choose citrus that's plump and gives a little when you squeeze it. Hard fruit won't produce much juice. Store citrus in the fridge to keep it fresh. To make batching easier, check your local market for fresh-pressed juice.

QUICK CONVERSIONS			
1 oz	⅛ c		
2 oz	¼ c		
4 oz	½ c		
8 oz	1 c	¼ qt	
16 oz	2 c	½ qt	
32 oz	4 c	1 qt	¼ gal
64 oz	8 c	2 qt	½ gal
128 oz	16 c	4 qt	1 gal

SPIRIT / WINE BOTTLE MEASUREMENTS		
375 ml	12 ½ oz	half bottle
750 ml	25 oz	standard bottle
1 L	34 oz	
1.5 L	50 oz	(2) 750 ml bottles
1.75 L	59 oz	

Bottles refer to USA standard sizes. EU standard sizes differ. Volumes are rounded for convenience and use the standard value of 8.115 US fluid ounces = 1 US legal cup = 1/4 US liquid quart.

FRUIT JUICE	
1 lemon	1 ½ oz juice
1 lime	1 oz juice
1 medium orange	3 oz juice
1 blood orange	2 oz juice
1 large grapefruit	8 oz juice

Average juice volume. Variety, size, season, growing location, weather conditions, and crop health impacts juice yield. Always purchase extra fruit to ensure you have enough juice for your recipe.

SIMPLE SYRUPS

These simple syrup recipes start out the same way—with a 1:1 ratio of sugar to water. The fun begins when you steep fruit, herbs, or spices to infuse flavor. These syrup recipes call for regular granulated sugar, but you can use turbinado or demerara sugar if you prefer, just know that the syrup will be brownish and will change the color of your cocktails.

SIMPLE SYRUP

8 oz sugar
8 oz water

Combine sugar and water in a small saucepan over high heat. Stir constantly to dissolve the sugar. Do not let it simmer. Remove from heat and cool the syrup to room temperature before storing.

STRAWBERRY SIMPLE SYRUP

8 oz sugar
8 oz water
8 fresh strawberries, hulled and quartered

Combine sugar and water in a small saucepan over high heat. Stir constantly to dissolve the sugar. Do not let it simmer. Remove from heat, then add strawberries, and let steep until the syrup cools to room temperature. Spoon out strawberry pieces before storing.

QUICK TIP
The microwave also works if you're in a hurry. Just heat 1 cup of water in a 4-cup glass measuring cup until boiling (about 5 minutes). Carefully remove from microwave and stir in 1 cup of sugar until it dissolves.

STORAGE
Keep syrup refrigerated in an air-tight container up to 2 weeks.

MEASUREMENT
8 ounces each of water and sugar makes about 12 ounces (1 ½ cups) of simple syrup. You can easily double the recipe for larger batches, or reduce the recipe if you need a smaller amount.

GINGER SIMPLE SYRUP

8 oz sugar
8 oz water
1 inch piece of ginger, peeled and thinly sliced
3 whole star anise
3 whole cloves

Use the back of a large knife to crack the spices and "wake" them. Combine sugar and water in a small saucepan over high heat. Stir constantly to dissolve the sugar. Do not let it simmer. Remove from heat. Add ginger and spices, and let steep until the syrup cools to room temperature. Pour the syrup through a strainer to remove all spices before storing.

LAVENDER SIMPLE SYRUP

8 oz sugar
8 oz water
2 tablespoons culinary lavender

Combine sugar and water in a small saucepan over high heat. Stir constantly to dissolve the sugar. Do not let it simmer. Remove from heat, then add lavender, and let steep until the syrup cools to room temperature. Pour the syrup through a strainer to remove lavender pieces before storing.

BASIL SIMPLE SYRUP

8 oz sugar
8 oz water
3 basil sprigs

Combine sugar and water in a small saucepan over high heat. Stir constantly to dissolve the sugar. Do not let it simmer. Remove from heat, then add basil sprigs, and let steep until the syrup cools to room temperature. Remove basil before storing.

JASMINE SIMPLE SYRUP

8 oz sugar
8 oz water
2 jasmine tea bags

Combine sugar and water in a small saucepan over high heat. Stir constantly to dissolve the sugar. Do not let it simmer. Remove from heat, then add tea bags, and let steep until the syrup cools to room temperature. Remove tea before storing.

ROSEMARY SIMPLE SYRUP

8 oz sugar
8 oz water
6 rosemary sprigs

Combine sugar and water in a small saucepan over high heat. Stir constantly to dissolve the sugar. Do not let it simmer. Remove from heat, then add rosemary sprigs, and let steep until the syrup cools to room temperature. Remove rosemary sprigs before storing.

CHAI SIMPLE SYRUP

8 oz sugar

8 oz water

1 inch piece of ginger, peeled and chopped

3 cardamom pods

1 star anise

1 cinnamon stick

8 black peppercorns

8 whole cloves

Use the back of a large knife to crack the spices and "wake" them. Combine sugar and water in a small saucepan over high heat. Stir constantly to dissolve the sugar. Do not let it simmer. Remove from heat, then add spices, and let steep until the syrup cools to room temperature. Pour the syrup through a strainer to remove all spices before storing.

CINNAMON SIMPLE SYRUP

8 oz sugar

8 oz water

2-3 cinnamon sticks

Use the back of a large knife to crack the cinnamon sticks and "wake" them. Add water and cinnamon to a small saucepan and bring to a boil over high heat. Add the sugar, stir constantly to dissolve and immediately remove from heat before it begins to simmer. Cover and let steep up about 12 hours Pour the syrup through a fine mesh strainer to remove all spices before storing.

JALAPEÑO SIMPLE SYRUP

8 oz sugar

8 oz water

2-3 jalapeños with seeds, sliced lengthwise

Combine sugar and water in a small saucepan over high heat. Stir constantly to dissolve the sugar. Do not let it simmer. Remove from heat, then add jalapeños. After 15 minutes, sample the syrup to test the spice level. Continue to steep, tasting every 15 minutes, until the syrup has achieved your desired spiciness. Pour the syrup through a strainer to remove jalapeños and seeds before storing.

MINT SIMPLE SYRUP

8 oz sugar

8 oz water

6 mint sprigs

Combine sugar and water in a small saucepan over high heat. Stir constantly to dissolve the sugar. Do not let it simmer. Remove from heat, then add mint sprigs, and let steep until the syrup cools to room temperature. Remove mint before storing.

GARNISH

When you're starting out, garnishes might seem fussy or optional. Technically, you can consume any cocktail in the book without added decoration, but garnishing your cocktail takes it from being a good drink to being a great drink. Have you ever heard the phrase, "We eat with our eyes first"? This is true for cocktails as well. The more appealing a drink looks, the better it tastes. Plus, garnishes don't only dress up a drink—many are vital ingredients that balance or enhance the flavor of each sip.

CITRUS

Citrus peel

Use a Y-peeler to remove the top layer of citrus. For a long peel, start at the very top and peel the rind vertically all the way to the bottom. Try to avoid the white pith. From here you have some options—add to the cocktail as is, trim the edges straight and the ends at an angle for an elegant appearance, or bend back and forth and place on a cocktail pick. For a citrus disc, remove a 2-inch section of peel. Place into the cocktail glass or gently bend disc in half and balance on the edge of the glass.

Expressed citrus oil

Some recipes call for squeezing a citrus peel over the finished cocktail, which covers the drink in a fine mist of citrus oil. To do this, hold the peel horizontally with the skin side facing down over your drink, then quickly squeeze as if bending the peel in half horizontally. You should see the fine spray of essential oil and smell its bright aroma. Do this a few times, then wipe the skin side of the peel around the outside edge of the glass. Drop peel into the cocktail glass to garnish.

Flaming citrus oil

Not only does this make for some fun theatrics, it also adds a hint of smokiness and deep caramel flavor to the citrus oil. Strike a match and hold the flame over the cocktail.

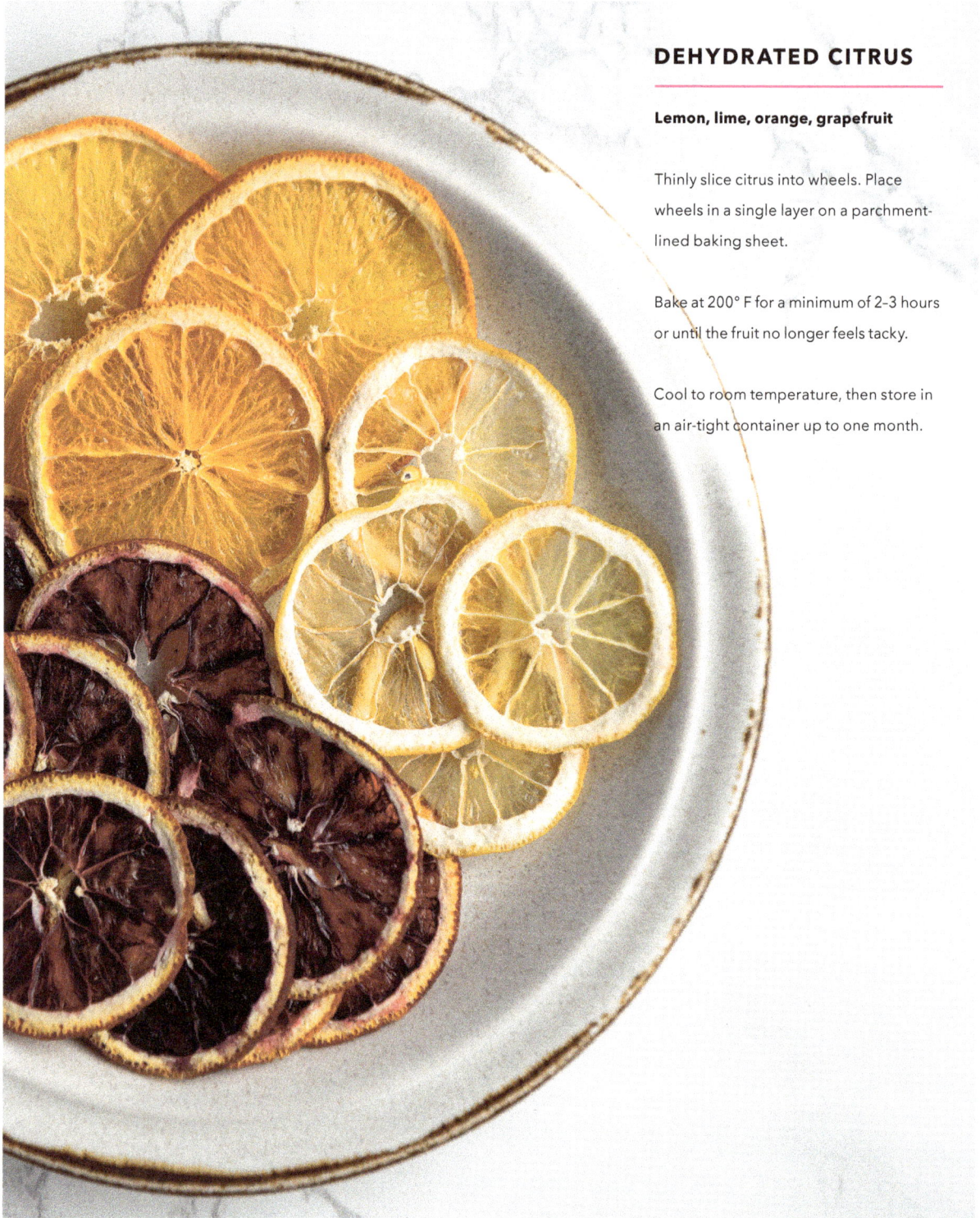

DEHYDRATED CITRUS

Lemon, lime, orange, grapefruit

Thinly slice citrus into wheels. Place wheels in a single layer on a parchment-lined baking sheet.

Bake at 200° F for a minimum of 2-3 hours or until the fruit no longer feels tacky.

Cool to room temperature, then store in an air-tight container up to one month.

With your other hand, squeeze the peel over the match to release the essential oil. You'll know that the oil made contact with the fire when you see a flash flame. Wipe the skin side of the peel around the outside edge of the glass. Drop peel into the cocktail glass.

Citrus twist or curl

Remove the citrus rind with the Y-peeler and trim edges if desired. Then, hold opposite ends of the peel, twist over the cocktail, and gently pull in opposite directions. If you'd like a longer peel or more dramatic twist, you can peel the citrus horizontally around the surface, instead of vertically from top to bottom. Twist, curl peel around your finger, then gently pull ends in opposite directions. Add to edge of cocktail glass.

Citrus wheel

Slice fruit crosswise into ¼-inch thick wheels. Place directly into drink or cut a small slit in the wheel so it can slide onto the edge of your cocktail glass. If your cocktail glass is small or your fruit is very large, cut the wheel in half.

Dehydrated citrus

I like to keep a stock of dehydrated citrus (page 19) on hand because it's a versatile and beautiful garnish that keeps well.

HERBS

Prepping herbs

After purchasing, immediately wash herbs and trim ends. Place in a plastic bag with a damp paper towel and refrigerate overnight. This allows the herbs time to absorb water and plump up. Otherwise your cocktail might have a wilted, floppy garnish. When setting up for a party, place herb sprigs in a short glass with just enough water to cover the stems.

Slapping mint

A mint sprig garnish looks great, but the fresh aroma actually enhances each sip of a cocktail. Before garnishing, wake up the herb and intensify the scent by slapping the mint sprig across your opposite hand.

CHERRIES

In my opinion, the best cocktail cherries you can buy are Luxardo. The small, firm cherries packed in a thick sour-sweet syrup elevates a variety of cocktails. My second choice would be Toschi because they are slightly smaller and they aren't quite as firm. Both will set you back $15 to $20 and are worth it. If you can't bring yourself to splurge, please don't reach for the neon red cherries of our youth. Read the label—you can find jars without artificial food coloring for around $8.

TEQUILA

PROPER MARGARITA FOR ONE

SWEET VS. SOUR

If you prefer a dry margarita, omit the simple syrup, and increase the Cointreau to 1 ounce. You'll still get a little sweetness from the Cointreau to balance out the tartness of the lime juice.

Substitute agave nectar in place of simple syrup to add depth to the finish. It is much sweeter than simple syrup so be sure to start with ¼ ounce and add more to taste.

ICE

Margaritas are often served over a glass full of ice cubes. I prefer mine with one large cube or straight up for a more intense flavor.

2 oz blanco tequila
½ oz Cointreau
1 oz lime juice (reserve one squeezed lime half)
½ oz simple syrup (page 13)
Lime wheel, for garnish

Combine tequila, lime juice, Cointreau, and simple syrup in a cocktail shaker filled with ice. Shake well until very cold, about 20 seconds.

Rub the edge of a rocks glass with reserved lime, then sprinkle salt on edge. Knock off extra salt from the edge and any that got inside of the glass. Add one large ice cube to the glass.

Strain cocktail into the salt-rimmed glass and garnish with a lime wheel.

PROPER MARGARITA

59 oz | 7 ¼ c | 2 qt

My cocktail journey began with my grandmother (MeMaw) and a salt-rimmed margarita. When I was eight years old, my grandparents organized regular dinners with family and friends at their favorite local Tex-Mex restaurant, El Jarro de Arturo, where I watched them sip margaritas, talk, and laugh for hours. When they weren't looking, I would run my finger along the rim of their glass to steal the salt for myself. They would always catch me, and we'd all laugh. It's my favorite childhood memory. A perfect moment in time. My grandparents are now gone, but the San Antonio restaurant is still popular today. Whenever I visit, I can feel their presence lingering in the audible laughter bouncing off the mirrored walls, and in every sip of the salt-rimmed margarita. At the end of my grandmother's life, I had the privilege of making her my own "proper margarita." I was no longer her eight-year-old granddaughter stealing the salt. I was a woman now. So we clinked glasses and shared one last perfect moment.

750 ml bottle blanco tequila

6 oz Cointreau

12 oz lime juice (reserve one squeezed lime half)

6 oz simple syrup (page 13)

10 oz water

Lime wheels, for garnish

Combine tequila, lime juice, Cointreau, simple syrup, and water in a beverage dispenser or pitcher. Chill until ready to serve.

To prep glasses, rub the edge of each rocks glass with reserved lime, then press edge into a dish filled with salt. Knock off extra salt from the edge and any that got inside of the glass.

When ready to serve, add one large ice cube to each glass. Stir cocktail before serving. Garnish with lime wheels.

DOUBLE BATCH (30 SERVINGS)

You can't go wrong with this universally loved cocktail, so mix up an extra large batch for your next gathering.

1.75 L blanco tequila

14 oz Cointreau

30 oz lime juice

14 oz simple syrup (page 13)

20 oz water

Lime wheels, for garnish

CITRUS JUICE

12 limes = 12 oz juice

30 limes = 30 oz juice

FRESH JUICE

Fresh-squeezed grapefruit juice will always taste better than the stuff in the carton. Try different varieties, such as Ruby Red, Oroblanco, Pink, Pomelo, and Thompson.

If you're in a pinch, check your local store for fresh-pressed, unpasteurized grapefruit juice.

INGREDIENT SWAP

The jalapeño simple syrup adds a slight kick, but if you're not feeling the heat, use classic, unflavored simple syrup.

2 oz blanco tequila

2 oz grapefruit juice

½ oz lime juice (reserve one squeezed lime half)

½ oz jalapeño simple syrup (page 17)

1 oz sparkling water

Grapefruit slice & jalapeño wheel, for garnish

Combine tequila, grapefruit juice, lime juice, and simple syrup in a cocktail shaker filled with ice. Shake well, about 20 seconds.

Rub the edge of a glass with the reserved lime, then sprinkle salt on edge. Empty out any salt that made its way into the glass. Fill glass with crushed ice.

Strain cocktail into salt-rimmed glass. Garnish with a grapefruit slice and jalapeño wheel.

PALOMA

61 oz | 7 ½ c | 1 ½ qt

Paloma is the Spanish word for "dove" and this drink's popularity spans countries and cultures. Most recipes call for grapefruit-flavored soda such as Fresca, Squirt, or Jarritos. I've replaced the flavored soda with a combo of fresh grapefruit juice and sparkling water for a refreshing cocktail you and your guests will want year-round.

750 ml bottle blanco tequila

24 oz grapefruit juice

6 oz lime juice (reserve one squeezed lime half)

6 oz jalapeño simple syrup (page 17)

12 oz sparkling water

Grapefruit slices & jalapeño wheels, for garnish

Combine tequila, grapefruit juice, lime juice, and simple syrup in a beverage dispenser or pitcher. Chill until ready to serve.

To prep glasses, rub the edge of each glass with reserved lime, then press edge into a dish filled with salt. Knock off extra salt from the edge and any that got inside of the glass.

When ready to serve, add sparkling water to batch cocktail, and stir to combine. Fill glasses with crushed ice and cocktail. Garnish with grapefruit slices and jalapeño wheels.

**DOUBLE BATCH
(30 SERVINGS)**

1.75 L blanco tequila

60 oz grapefruit juice

15 oz lime juice

14 oz jalapeño simple syrup (page 17)

30 oz sparkling water

Grapefruit slices & jalapeño wheels, for garnish

CITRUS JUICE

3 grapefruit = 24 oz juice
8 grapefruit = 64 oz juice

PINEAPPLE RESPITE

FOR ONE

1 ½ oz mezcal

½ oz blanco tequila

2 oz pineapple juice

½ oz lime juice (reserve one squeezed lime half)

½ simple syrup (page 13)

Pineapple slice, for garnish

Cilantro, for recipe and garnish

Muddle simple syrup and a couple of cilantro sprigs in a cocktail shaker. Add mezcal, tequila, pineapple juice, lime juice, and simple syrup. Fill with ice and shake about 20 seconds. Rub the edge of a glass with reserved lime, then sprinkle salt on edge. Strain cocktail into glass with one large ice cube. Garnish with pineapple slice and cilantro sprig.

Batch

12 SERVINGS 66 oz | 8 ¼ c | 1 ¾ qt

18 oz mezcal

6 oz blanco tequila

24 oz pineapple juice

6 oz lime juice (reserve one squeezed lime half)

6 simple syrup (page 13)

6 oz water

Pineapple slices, for garnish

Cilantro, for recipe and garnish

Muddle simple syrup and a handful of cilantro in a large pitcher, then add tequila, mezcal, juices, and water. Strain out cilantro and chill until ready to serve. Rub the edge of each glass with reserved lime, then press edge into a dish filled with salt. Add one large ice cube to each glass. Before serving, stir cocktail well. Garnish with pineapple slices and cilantro sprigs.

RECIPE TIP

Blending mezcal and tequila allows a bit of the smokiness from the mezcal to come forward without being too overpowering.

If you're drawn to smoky, peaty scotches, you might enjoy mixing up this recipe with only mezcal. If you're looking for less campfire flavor, the recipe is just as tasty with only tequila.

CILANTRO

This herb is wonderful for its numerous health benefits, but it's also a polarizing flavor. The cilantro plays a subtle role in this recipe, but if it's not your thing, leave it out.

FRUIT JUICE

If you have the time and energy to juice a pineapple, you should do it—you'll have an incredibly tasty drink. But, bottled pineapple juice is one of my exceptions to the fresh-is-better rule. I like to keep a stock of mini cans in my fridge for when the cocktail mood strikes.

SMOKE & FIRE

FOR ONE

1½ oz jalapeño-infused blanco tequila

½ oz mezcal

½ oz Cointreau

1 oz lime juice (reserve one squeezed lime half)

½ oz simple syrup (page 13)

Tajín or other chile salt, for rim

Lime wheel, for garnish

Combine ingredients in a cocktail shaker filled with ice, and shake about 20 seconds. Rub the edge of a glass with reserved lime half, then sprinkle chile salt on edge. Strain cocktail into a glass filled with cubed ice. Garnish.

Batch
16 SERVINGS   69 oz | 8 ½ c | 2 ¼ qt

750 ml jalapeño-infused blanco tequila

8 oz mezcal

8 oz Cointreau

16 oz lime juice (reserve one squeezed lime half)

8 oz simple syrup (page 13)

12 oz water

Tajín or other chile salt, for rim

Lime wheels, for garnish

Combine ingredients in a beverage dispenser and chill. To prep glasses, rub the edge of each glass with reserved lime, then press edge into a dish filled with chile salt. Fill glasses with cubed ice. Stir cocktail before serving. Garnish with lime wheels.

JALAPEÑO-INFUSED TEQUILA

For one

8 oz blanco tequila

½ jalapeño, julienne

For the batch

750 ml bottle blanco tequila

2 jalapeños, julienne

Add jalapeños to the bottle of tequila or a jar with lid. Shake well. Sample every 8 hours until the desired spice level is achieved. Once infused, strain out the peppers and seeds.

SPICE OPTIONS

There are many ways to make a spicy margarita, so experiment with what you have on hand. Instead of infusing the tequila, try:

- *Substitute ½ ounce Ancho Reyes in place of Cointreau*
- *2 dashes of Scrappy's Firewater bitters*
- *Jalapeño simple syrup (page 17)*
- *Muddle a few jalapeño slices with tequila. For less heat, strain out the peppers and seeds before mixing the rest of the cocktail.*

MIDWINTER BREAK `FOR ONE`

---

2 oz blanco tequila

½ oz Cointreau

1½ oz blood orange juice

1 oz lime juice

½ oz simple syrup (page 13)

Blood orange wheel, for garnish

Combine tequila, blood orange juice, lime juice, Cointreau, and simple syrup in a cocktail shaker filled with ice. Shake well until very cold, about 20 seconds.

Rub the edge of a glass with reserved lime, then sprinkle salt on edge. Empty out any salt that made its way into the glass, then fill with crushed ice.

Strain cocktail into salt-rimmed glass. Garnish with a blood orange wheel.

MIDWINTER BREAK

70 oz | 8 ¾ c | 2 ¼ qt

Blood oranges are at their peak during the dreary, winter months, which is why I love the bright, transformative color they bring to drinks. The intense red pigment that makes cocktails look beautiful contains antioxidants, and citrus is rich in vitamin C, so each sip provides "healthy" benefits!

750 ml bottle blanco tequila

6 oz Cointreau

18 oz blood orange juice

12 oz lime juice (reserve one squeezed lime half)

6 oz simple syrup (page 13)

3 oz water

Blood orange wheels, for garnish

Combine tequila, blood orange juice, lime juice, Cointreau, simple syrup, and water in a beverage dispenser or pitcher. Chill until ready to serve.

To prep glasses, rub the edge of each glass with reserved lime then press edge into a dish filled with salt. Empty out any salt that made its way into the glass.

When ready to serve, fill glasses with crushed ice. Stir cocktail shortly before serving. Garnish with blood orange wheels.

**DOUBLE BATCH
(24 SERVINGS)**

1.75 L blanco tequila

10 oz Cointreau

36 oz blood orange juice

24 oz lime juice

10 oz simple syrup (page 13)

8 oz water

CITRUS JUICE
9 blood oranges = 18 oz juice
18 blood oranges = 36 oz juice

FIRE IN THE SKY

2 oz blanco tequila

2 oz mango juice (or puree)

½ oz lemon juice

1 dash Scrappy's Firewater bitters (optional)

Dehydrated blood orange wheel, for garnish (page 19)

Add all ingredients to shaker with ice. Shake well until cold and combined. Double strain into a coupe glass and serve straight up. Garnish with a dehydrated blood orange wheel.

Batch

12 SERVINGS

63 oz | 7 ¾ c | 2 qt

750 ml bottle blanco tequila

24 oz mango juice (or puree)

6 oz lemon juice

8 oz water

12 dashes Scrappy's Firewater bitters (optional)

Dehydrated blood orange wheels, for garnish (page 19)

Combine ingredients in a beverage dispenser or pitcher and chill. Stir cocktail before serving, then pour into coupe glasses. Garnish with dehydrated blood orange wheels.

MANGO JUICE

While fresh-squeezed juice is usually best, making mango juice at home takes a lot of effort unless you have a high-speed juicer. If you don't have access to one, purchase mango juice from a grocery store.

MODIFICATION

Scrappy's Firewater bitters adds a spicy kick and pairs well with the sweetness of the mango juice. If you're not a fan of spicy drinks, you can leave it out without impacting the flavor.

WHISKEY

OLD FASHIONED `FOR ONE`

2 oz bourbon or rye

¼ oz simple syrup (page 13)

2 dashes orange bitters

1 dash Angostura bitters

Orange peel, for garnish

Cocktail cherry, for garnish

Combine bourbon, simple syrup, and bitters in a mixing glass. Fill with ice and stir with cocktail mixing spoon for about 20 seconds, until very cold.

Strain cocktail into a rocks glass with one large ice cube.

Remove a long piece of orange peel. With the outer peel facing over the cocktail, squeeze quickly to release essential oils.

Garnish drink with orange peel and cherry.

GARNISH

Don't skip this part. It might seem like it's just for show, but the orange essence and peel transform this from a good drink into a really amazing cocktail.

VARIATIONS

Try adding a few different types of bitters:
- *Add 1 dash of Peychaud's bitters to the orange and Angostura bitters*
- *Add 2 dashes of Old Fashioned bitters (and remove the other bitters)*

SAZERAC

2 oz rye

½ oz simple syrup (page 13)

3 dashes Peychaud's bitters

1 dash Angostura bitters

Absinthe rinse

Lemon peel, for garnish

Stir ingredients with ice for 20 seconds. Pour or spritz a small amount of absinthe into an empty rocks glass. Swirl it around to coat the sides and discard the extra. Add cocktail, then garnish.

OLD FASHIONED

32 oz | 4 cups | 1 quart

The Old Fashioned is one of my favorite drinks. When made properly, it's an adaptable companion that spans activities and seasons. It is also a wonderful jumping off point for countless variations. Your favorite barkeep might serve it muddled with a neon cherry and orange wedge, or in a glass filled to the brim with ice or sparkling water. But, before you settle into those adaptations, please give this recipe a try.

750 ml bottle bourbon or rye

3 oz simple syrup (page 13)

20 dashes orange bitters

10 dashes Angostura bitters

4 oz water

12 orange peels (from 2-3 oranges), for garnish

24 cocktail cherries, for garnish

Add bourbon, simple syrup, and water to beverage dispenser. Stir well and chill in fridge.

Remove long pieces of orange peel to garnish each drink. Cover with a damp cloth and set aside. Prep cocktail picks by adding cherries to each one.

Shortly before serving, add bitters to chilled cocktail and stir. Add one large ice cube to each rocks glass and pour cocktail.

To finish drink, hold an orange peel, outer side facing down over the glass, and quickly squeeze to release essential oils. Garnish with the orange peels and cherries.

BOTTLE IT

Homemade Old Fashioneds make a thoughtful gift for the cocktail enthusiast in your life. Purchase swing-top glass bottles online or at a local specialty store.

This batch recipe makes enough for two 16-ounce bottles. Dress up the bottle with a ribbon and handwritten tag (reminding the recipient to refrigerate) and you've got the perfect party host gift.

BLACK MANHATTAN

CLASSIC MANHATTAN

If you prefer a classic Manhattan cocktail, simply substitute a sweet vermouth, such as Cocchi Rosa or Dolin Rouge, in place of Averna.

2 oz bourbon or rye

1 oz sweet vermouth

1 dash orange bitters

1 dash Angostura bitters

3 cocktail cherries, for garnish

2 oz bourbon or rye

1 oz Averna

1 dash orange bitters

1 dash Angostura bitters

3 cocktail cherries, for garnish

Add rye, Averna, and bitters to a mixing glass with ice. Stir with cocktail mixing spoon for about 20 seconds, until very cold.

Strain into a coupe. Garnish with three cocktail cherries.

Put on some jazz and sip slowly.

BLACK MANHATTAN

43 oz | 5 ¼ c | 1 ¼ qt

The Manhattan is one of the most classic craft cocktails. It was created around 1880 at New York City's Manhattan Club, and has remained the same since. The Black Manhattan variation—created by bartender Todd Smith—uses Italian amaro in place of sweet vermouth. Amaro is an Italian liqueur flavored by herbs, spices, and botanicals, which make it a little more bitter. It blends well with bourbon and rye to produce a well-balanced and boozy take on the classic drink. This recipe calls for Averna, but try other amari and find your new favorite.

750 ml bottle bourbon or rye

12 oz Averna

10 dashes orange bitters

10 dashes Angostura bitters

6 oz water

36 cocktail cherries, for garnish

Add rye, Averna, and water to a carafe or beverage dispenser. Chill until ready to use.

Prep garnish by placing cherries on a cocktail picks.

Shortly before serving, add bitters to chilled cocktail and stir.

Pour cocktail into coupe glasses and garnish with cherries.

SWEETNESS

If you like your drinks on the sour side, reduce the simple syrup to ½ ounce, or increase the amount of lemon juice to 1 ounce.

CITRUS JUICE

There's no substitute for fresh lemon juice. The bottled version might seem tempting, but it changes the flavor of the cocktail.

Citrus stays fresh for a long time when refrigerated. Stock up and you'll always have fresh juice! Once you squeeze your fruit, use the juice within a day or two.

1½ oz bourbon or rye

1 oz strawberry simple syrup (page 13)

¾ oz lemon juice

1 dash Peychaud's bitters

2 dashes orange bitters

1 strawberry, for garnish

Mint sprig, for garnish

Add bourbon, strawberry simple syrup, lemon juice, and bitters to a shaker with ice. Shake vigorously for about 20 seconds.

Strain into a glass filled with crushed or cubed ice.

Garnish with strawberry and mint sprig.

SUMMER SOLSTICE

63 oz | 7 ¾ c | 2 qt

This cocktail is like summer in a glass. Bourbon mingles with lemon juice and in-season strawberries to create a bold yet refreshing punch. Fresh strawberries are only in season for a short time, but you can have that summertime feeling year-round—purchase ripe strawberries while they're in season, and freeze for later. Be sure to thaw them out before adding them to the simple syrup.

750 ml bottle bourbon or rye

16 oz strawberry simple syrup (page 13)

12 oz lemon juice

14 dashes Peychaud's bitters

30 dashes orange bitters

10 oz water

16 strawberries, for garnish

16 mint sprigs, for garnish

Combine bourbon, strawberry simple syrup, lemon juice, and water in beverage dispenser, and chill.

Prep garnish by adding a strawberry to each cocktail pick. Or, place a slit in the bottom half of small strawberries, if you prefer to place the garnish on the edge of the glass.

Shortly before serving, add bitters to chilled cocktail and stir. Fill glasses with crushed or cubed ice and pour cocktail.

Garnish with strawberry and mint.

RECIPE TIP

Booze, fruit juices, and simple syrups tend to separate shortly after mixing, so it's important to stir the cocktail in the beverage dispenser throughout the party to avoid an unbalanced drink.

CITRUS JUICE

8 lemons = 12 oz juice

PICARD

HERBAL NOTES

Not sure if you're a fan of lavender or bergamot? Try the recipe with unflavored bourbon, and infuse Earl Grey tea into the simple syrup instead of lavender. It will impart a very subtle Earl Grey flavor.

EARL GREY BOURBON

For one

8 oz bourbon
1 Earl Grey tea bag

For the batch

750 ml bottle bourbon
3 Earl Grey tea bags

Pour bourbon into a glass jar or container. Add tea bags and stir. Cover and let steep for 15 to 30 minutes, depending on desired flavor.

2 oz Earl Grey bourbon
½ oz lavender simple syrup (page 15)
½ oz lemon juice
2 dashes orange bitters
Lemon peel, for garnish

Combine Earl Grey bourbon, lavender simple syrup, and bitters in a shaker filled with ice. Shake for 20 seconds, until very cold.

Strain into a rocks glass with one large ice cube.

Remove a long piece of lemon peel, and trim edges straight. With the outer peel facing over the cocktail, squeeze quickly to release essential oils.

Twist lemon peel to curl, then garnish cocktail.

PICARD

43 oz | 5 ¼ c | 1 ¼ qt

The inspiration for this recipe comes from my love of sci-fi. I'm a pretty big Star Trek: The Next Generation nerd, and a big fan of Sir Patrick Stewart. I created this cocktail to celebrate the birthday of Sir Patrick Stewart and his STTNG character, Captain Jean-Luc Picard. They were born on the same day, 365 years apart. See, I'm a nerd. If you've ever watched STTNG, you'll know that Captain Picard's favorite drink is, "Tea. Earl Grey. Hot."

---

750 ml Earl Grey bourbon (page 56)

6 oz lavender simple syrup (page 15)

6 oz lemon juice

6 oz water

22 dashes orange bitters

Lemon peels (from about 3 lemons)**, for garnish**

Combine Earl Grey bourbon, lavender simple syrup, and water in a beverage dispenser. Chill until ready to use.

Remove long pieces of lemon peel to garnish each drink. Trim edges straight. Cover with a damp cloth and set aside.

Shortly before serving, add bitters to chilled cocktail and stir. Add one large ice cube to each rocks glass and pour cocktail.

To finish drink, hold a lemon peel, outer skin side down, over each glass and quickly squeeze to release essential oils. Then, twist peel to curl and garnish each cocktail.

Now, make it so!

MINT JULEP

SWEETNESS

This cocktail is equally boozy and sweet, but if you prefer cocktails with a subtle sweetness, reduce the mint simple syrup to ½ ounce and add a splash of water.

RECIPE TIP

The technique of building the Julep in the glass is quick and easy, just be sure to stir your cocktail before consuming so the ingredients are mixed and the flavor balanced.

RUM JULEP

Put a tiki twist on this southern favorite. Just swap the bourbon for dark rum.

2 oz dark rum

1 oz mint simple syrup (page 17)

1 cup crushed ice

Mint sprig, for garnish

2 oz bourbon

1 oz mint simple syrup (page 17)

Mint sprig, for garnish

Fill a highball glass or julep cup with crushed or shaved ice, then add the mint simple syrup.

Add bourbon and splash of water (optional), then add more ice to fill the glass.

Garnish with a mint sprig.

MINT JULEP

41 oz | 5 c | 1 ¼ qt

The Mint Julep is the official cocktail of the Kentucky Derby. Instead of the traditional method of muddling mint leaves, this recipe calls for mint-infused simple syrup. It's more user-friendly when batching cocktails for a Derby party, plus it's great to have on hand in case you need an impromptu bourbon drink.

750 ml bottle bourbon

12 oz mint simple syrup (page 17)

4 oz water

2 bunches of mint, for garnish

Add the bourbon, mint simple syrup, and water to a beverage dispenser. Stir to combine and chill.

To prep mint garnish, trim ends and place in a short glass of water to keep fresh.

Shortly before serving, crush or shave the ice (or save some time and buy a couple bags if you can find it).

When ready to serve, fill glasses with ice. Stir chilled cocktail and pour into glasses. Top each glass with more ice.

Garnish with mint sprigs.

DOUBLE BATCH (30 SERVINGS)

To serve this historic cocktail at your next party, I recommend preparing a double batch!

1.75 L bourbon

30 oz mint simple syrup (page 17)

6 oz water

4-5 bunches of mint, for garnish

KENTUCKY BOURBON

You can technically use your favorite house whiskey to craft the Mint Julep, but my go-to is always Woodford Reserve. It's still made in small batches in Kentucky.

HOT TODDY

After moving to Seattle, my husband and I gather a group of friends each winter and caravan to a Christmas tree farm. We trek across fields looking for the perfect tree, then toast to our friendship over hot toddies. Every time I sip a hot toddy on a cold night, I'm reminded of these special moments when we all stop, connect, and celebrate each other, before the madness of the holiday season begins. It's one of my favorite days of the year.

FOR ONE

2 oz bourbon

1 oz ginger simple syrup (page 13)

2 oz apple cider

½ oz lemon juice

Cinnamon stick, optional garnish

Combine all ingredients and microwave for 2 minutes or heat on the stove until steaming hot. Pour into a mug. Garnish with a cinnamon stick and serve immediately.

> **RECIPE TIP**
> *When purchasing apple cider, look on the label for the fewest ingredients. If the cider has added sugar, reduce the amount of simple syrup to taste.*
>
> *Your local farmers market is a great place to find fresh apple cider.*

Batch

12 SERVINGS 65 oz | 8 c | 2 qt

750 ml bottle bourbon

10 oz ginger simple syrup (page 13)

24 oz apple cider

6 oz lemon juice

Cinnamon sticks, optional garnish

Combine all ingredients in a large pot and heat on medium until steaming hot. Serve immediately, or transfer to an insulated growler or thermos. Garnish with cinnamon sticks.

NEWTON'S REFRAIN

CITRUS SWAP

Substitute any in-season orange if blood oranges aren't available. The flavor of oranges differs between varieties and where they're grown, so adjust the simple syrup to taste.

2 oz rye
½ oz chai simple syrup (page 16)
¾ oz blood orange juice
2 dashes Angostura bitters
2 cocktail cherries, for garnish

Combine rye, blood orange juice, simple syrup, and bitters in a cocktail shaker with ice. Shake for about 20 seconds.

Strain cocktail through a mesh strainer into a rocks glass with one large ice cube.

Garnish with cocktail cherries.

NEWTON'S REFRAIN

48 oz | 6 cups | 1 ½ quarts

The Newton name comes from my dad's side, and our family tree includes many talented musicians and songwriters. While I didn't inherit any musical talent, I'm pretty sure my dad passed down his love of whiskey. In this cocktail, blood orange juice and chai spices play with bourbon in perfect harmony for a cozy spin on the Old Fashioned. For a booze-forward option, omit the juice altogether.

750 ml bottle rye

6 oz chai simple syrup (page 16)

8 oz blood orange juice

8 oz water

20 dashes Angostura bitters

24 cocktail cherries, for garnish

RECIPE TIP

Straining the juice removes most of the pulp and keeps the beverage dispenser spout from getting blocked as you serve the cocktail.

CITRUS JUICE

4 blood oranges = 8 oz juice

Using hand-held juicer, squeeze orange juice into a measuring cup. Pour the orange juice through a mesh strainer into a second measuring cup until you have 8 ounces.

Add rye, orange juice, simple syrup, and water to beverage dispenser. Stir well and refrigerate until chilled.

Prep garnish by placing cherries on cocktail picks.

Shortly before serving, add bitters to the chilled cocktail and stir. Add one large ice cube to each rocks glass and pour cocktail.

Garnish with cocktail cherries.

VERMILION PUNCH FOR ONE

CITRUS SWAP

Substitute another variety of orange if blood oranges aren't available or in season. The cocktail won't have a red hue, but it will still taste great.

INGREDIENT SWAP

Instead of cinnamon simple syrup, use ½ ounce of Ancho Reyes and ¼ ounce of plain simple syrup, for a similar flavor with a hint of a spice.

2 oz bourbon

2 oz blood orange juice

½ oz cinnamon simple syrup (page 17)

1 oz sparkling wine, such as Prosecco or Cava

1 oz sparkling water

Blood orange wedge, for garnish

Mint sprig, for garnish

Add bourbon, blood orange juice, and simple syrup to a shaker filled with ice. Shake well to combine, about 20 seconds.

Strain cocktail through mesh strainer into a glass filled with crushed or cubed ice.

Top with sparkling wine and sparkling water.

Garnish with a blood orange wedge and mint sprig.

VERMILION PUNCH

91 oz | 11 ¼ cups | 2 ¾ quarts

This cocktail packs a punch in more ways than one! Vermilion is a blood-red pigment, like the color of a Moro blood orange, which lends its dramatic hue to this eye-catching punch. Serve it at holiday parties, when blood oranges are in season, or substitute another orange variety for year-round enjoyment.

750 ml bottle bourbon

24 oz blood orange juice

6 oz cinnamon simple syrup (page 17)

12 oz sparkling wine, such as Prosecco or Cava

24 oz sparkling water, chilled

Blood orange wedges, for garnish

Mint leaves, for garnish

Add blood orange juice, bourbon, and simple syrup to a beverage dispenser or punch bowl. Stir to combine and chill until ready to serve.

Shortly before serving, stir the punch, then add the sparkling wine and sparkling water.

Fill glasses with crushed or cubed ice, then add the cocktail.

Garnish with blood orange wedges and mint leaves.

RECIPE TIP

Booze, fruit juices, and simple syrups tend to separate shortly after mixing, so it's important to stir the cocktail throughout the party to avoid an unbalanced drink.

CITRUS JUICE

12 blood oranges = 24 oz juice

Purchase a few extra oranges to use as garnish.

VODKA

On the Terrace
SINGLE & BATCH 75

Moscow Mule
SINGLE 78 · **BATCH** 79

House of Underdown
SINGLE 82 · **BATCH** 83

Bowling Partner
SINGLE & BATCH 85

Evening Stroll
SINGLE 88 · **BATCH** 89

Obvious Friend
SINGLE & BATCH 91

ON THE TERRACE

The herbaceous flavors in Green Chartreuse and rosemary simple syrup mingle with vodka and sparkling water for a new spin on the traditional vodka tonic. It's crisp enough to serve year-round but it has enough depth to drink in colder months, and it can hold its own next to your favorite bourbon cocktail.

FOR ONE

2 oz vodka

1 oz Green Chartreuse

1 oz rosemary simple syrup (page 15)

2 dashes Angostura bitters

4 oz sparkling water

Rosemary sprig & lemon wheel, for garnish

Combine vodka, Green Chartreuse, simple syrup, and bitters in a shaker with ice. Shake until cold. Strain into a highball glass filled with cubed ice. Top with sparkling water. Garnish with rosemary sprig and lemon wheel.

Batch

25 SERVINGS

200 oz | 24 ¾ c | 6 ¼ qt

(2) 750 ml bottles of vodka

750 ml bottle Green Chartreuse

25 oz rosemary simple syrup (page 15)

45 dashes (or ¾ oz) Angostura bitters

3 liters sparkling water

Rosemary sprigs & lemon wheels, for garnish

Add vodka, Green Chartreuse, and simple syrup to a beverage dispenser. Refrigerate until chilled. When ready to serve, add sparkling water and bitters to chilled cocktail and stir. Fill highball glasses with cubed ice. Pour cocktail into glasses and garnish with rosemary sprigs and lemon wheels.

SPARKLING WATER VS. TONIC WATER

I prefer sparkling water because it's easy to find at any store and comes in dozens of calorie-free flavors. Look for bottles without juice or artificial additives. This recipe calls for unflavored sparkling water, but it would also be tasty with lemon or grapefruit flavored water.

Tonic contains sugar or corn syrup to balance its bitter flavor. If you prefer it over sparkling water, be sure to adjust the amount of simple syrup and bitters to taste.

2 oz vodka

½ oz lime juice (save squeezed lime half for garnish)

6 oz ginger beer

½ oz simple syrup (page 13)

Combine all ingredients in a shaker filled with ice. Gently shake until cold. Let sit for a minute so the ginger beer doesn't erupt, then carefully open shaker.

Strain cocktail into a copper mug filled with cubed ice.

Press up on the bottom of the squeezed lime half to turn it inside out, and garnish cocktail.

DARK & STORMY

To make this classic, simply swap the vodka for dark rum.

2 oz dark rum

½ oz lime juice
(save squeezed lime half)

3 oz ginger beer

½ oz simple syrup
(page 13)

OAXACA MULE

Smoky mezcal and spicy ginger are a perfect pair.

2 oz mezcal or tequila

½ oz lime juice
(save squeezed lime half)

3 oz ginger beer

½ oz simple syrup
(page 13)

MOSCOW MULE

109 oz | 13 ½ c | 3 ½ qt

This refreshing crowd favorite is traditionally served in a copper mug to keep it ice-cold. The exact origins of the Moscow Mule are somewhat debated. The story goes that in the 1940s the owner of Smirnoff couldn't sell vodka. He met a bar owner who couldn't sell homemade ginger beer. One day, a woman walked into the bar peddling the copper mugs she made in Russia (but couldn't sell), and the rest is cocktail history.

750 ml bottle vodka

6 oz lime juice (save squeezed limes for garnish)

72 oz ginger beer

6 oz simple syrup (page 13)

After juicing limes, press up on the bottom of the each squeezed half to turn it inside out. Place limes in an airtight bag, and freeze.

Add vodka, lime juice, ginger beer, and simple syrup to a beverage dispenser and chill.

When ready to serve, fill copper mugs (or your favorite glassware) with cubed ice. Stir chilled cocktail and pour.

Garnish each mug with a frozen lime half.

GINGER BEER VS. GINGER ALE

Ginger beer is naturally fermented, but it's still considered a non-alcoholic drink. It has a more intense ginger flavor than ginger ale, which is carbonated water with ginger flavoring. When choosing ginger beer, check the label. If it contains a large amount of sugar, you might find you don't need any simple syrup in the recipe.

DOUBLE BATCH (30 SERVINGS)

This easy-drinking cocktail is always a big hit, so you'll probably want to make a double batch. Take it to a party, on a camping trip, or be really well stocked when family comes to visit.

1.75 L vodka

15 oz lime juice

180 oz ginger beer

15 oz simple syrup (page 13)

HOUSE OF UNDERDOWN

2 oz vodka

½ oz St~Germain

1 oz grapefruit juice

½ oz lemon juice

½ oz lime juice

½ oz simple syrup (page 13)

Grapefruit disc, for garnish

Combine vodka, St~Germain, citrus juices, and simple syrup in a shaker filled with ice. Shake for 20 seconds, until very cold.

Strain into a Nick & Nora glass or a small coupe.

Remove a 2-inch piece of grapefruit peel. With the outer skin facing down over the cocktail, quickly squeeze to release essential oils. Then, gently bend in half and garnish cocktail.

HOUSE OF UNDERDOWN

64 oz | 8 c | 2 qt

I met Perry and Angela Underdown shortly after moving to Seattle from Texas. Like most residents in the city, they were also recent transplants. Angela grew up down the road in Portland. Perry was raised in the South and has family in Texas. At the time, it was rare to run into urban liberals from the South, so we instantly bonded over shared experiences, and cocktails, of course. As we navigated our new city, Angela, Perry, and their son Charlie Tex became the foundation of our Seattle family. They have been massive supporters of this book from the beginning, and I can always count on them to sample new recipes.

750 ml bottle vodka

5 oz St~Germain

12 oz grapefruit juice

6 oz lemon juice

6 oz lime juice

4 oz simple syrup (page 13)

10 oz water

Grapefruit discs, for garnish

CITRUS JUICE
2 grapefruit = 16 oz juice
4 lemons = 6 oz juice
6 limes = 6 oz juice

Before juicing the grapefruit, remove 2-inch pieces of peel to garnish each drink. Cover with a damp cloth and set aside.

Combine vodka, St~Germain, citrus juices, simple syrup, and water in a beverage dispenser or pitcher. Chill until ready to use.

When ready to serve, stir the cocktail, and pour into Nick & Nora glasses or small coupes.

To finish each drink, hold a grapefruit disc, with the outer skin side down, over the glass and quickly squeeze to release essential oils. Then, gently bend in half and garnish cocktail.

BOWLING PARTNER

This variation of The Dude's favorite libation was inspired by the iced chai latte. With only three ingredients it's easy to mix up so you can just chill, man.

FOR ONE

2 oz chai-spiced vodka

1 oz coffee liqueur

1 oz half-and-half

Add chai-spiced vodka, coffee liqueur, and half-and-half to a shaker with ice. Shake for 20 seconds, until very cold. Strain into a rocks glass filled with cubed ice.

Batch

12 SERVINGS

59 oz | 7 ¼ c | 1 ¾ qt

750 ml chai-spiced vodka

12 oz coffee liqueur

12 oz half-and-half

10 oz water

In a pitcher, combine chai-spiced vodka, coffee liqueur, half-and-half, and water. Refrigerate until very cold.

Shortly before serving, fill rocks glasses with cubed ice. Stir chilled cocktail and pour into glasses.

CHAI-SPICED VODKA

For one

6 oz vodka

3 cardamom pods

1 star anise pods

1 cinnamon stick

For the batch

750 ml bottle of bourbon

9 cardamom pods

3 star anise pods

2 cinnamon sticks

Crush spices with the back of a knife to "wake" them. Add vodka and spices together in a glass bottle. Cover and let the vodka infuse overnight. Strain out the spices before using.

EVENING STROLL

2 oz vodka

1 oz jasmine simple syrup (page 15)

½ oz lemon juice

2 oz sparkling water

Candied lemon wheel, for garnish

Combine vodka, jasmine simple syrup, and lemon juice in a cocktail shaker filled with ice. Shake for 20 seconds until chilled.

Strain into a glass filled with cubed ice. Top with sparkling water, to taste. Garnish with candied lemon wheel.

EVENING STROLL

67 oz | 8 ¼ c | 2 qt

This cocktail reminds me of strolling through my neighborhood during summer evenings when the sweet smell of blooming jasmine hangs in the air. The simple syrup is infused with jasmine tea which imparts subtle floral notes to this light and freshing drink.

750 ml bottle vodka

12 oz jasmine simple syrup (page 15)

6 oz lemon juice

24 oz sparkling water

Candied lemon wheels, for garnish

Combine vodka, jasmine simple syrup, and lemon juice in a beverage dispenser or pitcher and chill.

When ready to serve, fill glasses with cubed ice. Stir the chilled cocktail, and add sparkling water to taste, then pour into glasses.

Garnish with candied lemon wheels.

OBVIOUS FRIEND

Although this cocktail only contains one ingredient—making it the easiest recipe in the book—it's still packed full of flavor. The sugar and acid from the pineapple juice mellows out the vodka, leaving you with a naturally sweet martini that goes down very smooth.

FOR ONE

3 oz pineapple vodka
Lemon peel, for garnish

Add pineapple-infused vodka to a shaker filled with ice. Shake vigorously for 20 seconds. Strain into a martini glass. Remove a long piece of lemon peel. With the outer skin facing down over the cocktail, quickly squeeze to release essential oils. Garnish.

PINEAPPLE VODKA

750 ml bottle vodka
1 fresh pineapple

Peel, core, and cube fresh pineapple. Add pineapple to an airtight glass jar, then pour in vodka. Seal and refrigerate 5-7 days. Shake or stir daily and sample. The vodka is ready when it takes on the sweetness of the pineapple. Then, strain out the fruit chunks. Don't be tempted to eat the boozy pineapple—all the delicious goodness has been sucked out of the fruit. It tastes disgusting, trust me! Store infused vodka in the fridge for up to 2 weeks.

Batch

8 SERVINGS

30 oz | 3 ¾ c | 1 qt

750 ml pineapple vodka
6 oz water
Lemon peel (from 2 lemons)**, for garnish**

Combine pineapple-infused vodka and water in a serving pitcher and chill until ice-cold. When ready to serve, stir cocktail and pour into glasses. To finish drink, remove long pieces of lemon peel. Hold a lemon peel, outer skin side down, over the glass and quickly squeeze to release essential oils. Garnish.

GIN

FRENCH 75

The bubbly cocktail that feels retro and glamorous at the same time. It's versatile enough to drink at brunch or happy hour. Some historians say this classic was created in 1915, Paris. Named after the French 75mm field gun used in World War I, because it packed a powerful punch. While cocktail purists debate over using gin or cognac, I've included both versions so you can decide for yourself!

FOR ONE

1 ¼ oz gin

3 oz Champagne Brut, or dry sparkling wine

½ oz lemon juice

½ oz simple syrup (page 13)

Lemon peel, for garnish

Add gin, lemon juice, and simple syrup to a shaker filled with ice. Shake until cold, then strain into champagne flute and top with sparkling wine. Garnish with a lemon peel.

SPIRIT SWAP

If you're a whiskey drinker, you might prefer this richer cognac variation, that some say is the original recipe.

1 ¼ oz cognac

3 oz Champagne Brut, or dry sparkling wine

½ oz lemon juice

½ oz simple syrup (page 13)

Lemon peel, for garnish

Batch

10 SERVINGS

45 oz | 5 ½ cups | 1 ½ quarts

10 oz gin

750 ml bottle Champagne Brut, or dry sparkling wine

4 oz lemon juice

4 oz simple syrup (page 13)

2 oz of water

Lemon peel, for garnish

Add gin, lemon juice, simple syrup, and water to a pitcher. Chill until cold. When ready to serve, remove a long piece of lemon peel for each glass. Stir cocktail and pour roughly 2 ¼ ounces into each champagne flute. Top each glass with 3 ounces of sparkling wine. Garnish with lemon peels.

GREYHOUND RESCUE

The original Greyhound cocktail has fallen in and out of popularity since its conception in the 1930s, but this variation is one of my favorite drinks to serve when entertaining. The rosemary simple syrup imparts complex herbaceous notes, and the sweetness rounds out the tart grapefruit juice. Gin adds floral notes and more depth of flavor, but the recipe can also be made with vodka.

2 oz gin

½ oz rosemary simple syrup (page 15)

4 oz grapefruit juice

Rosemary sprig, for garnish

Grapefruit wedge, for garnish

Add gin, rosemary simple syrup, and grapefruit juice to a shaker filled with ice. Shake for 20 seconds and strain into glass filled with cubed ice. Garnish with a grapefruit wedge and rosemary sprig.

Batch

12 SERVINGS

87 oz | 10 ¾ c | 2 ¾ qt

750 ml bottle of gin

6 oz rosemary simple syrup (page 15)

48 oz grapefruit juice

8 oz water

2 bunches rosemary sprigs, for garnish

1 grapefruit, cut into wedges, for garnish

Add gin, rosemary simple syrup, grapefruit juice, and water to beverage dispenser and chill. Fill glasses with cubed ice. Before serving, stir chilled cocktail and pour into glasses. Garnish with grapefruit slices and rosemary sprigs.

DOUBLE BATCH (30 SERVINGS)

This is always a crowd favorite, so I suggest mixing up a double batch!

1.75 L gin

15 oz rosemary simple syrup (page 15)

120 oz grapefruit juice

20 oz water

5 bunches rosemary, for garnish

2 grapefruit, cut into wedges, for garnish

CITRUS JUICE

6 grapefruit = 48 oz juice
15 grapefruit = 120 oz juice

HERBAL NOTES

Experiment with other herbal simple syrups, like basil and lavender (both on page 15). These aromatic botanicals naturally complement grapefruit and gin.

BOULEVARDIER

Try whiskey in place of gin for a rich and intriguing variation of the Negroni.

1 oz bourbon or rye

1 oz Campari

1 oz sweet vermouth

Orange twist or slice, for garnish

1 oz gin

1 oz Campari

1 oz sweet vermouth

Orange twist or slice, for garnish

Stir all ingredients in a mixing glass with ice until very cold, about 20 seconds.

Strain into a rocks glass with one large ice cube, or serve straight up in a coupe glass.

Garnish with an orange twist or slice.

NEGRONI

91 oz | 11 ¼ c | 2 ¾ qt

The Negroni is the easiest recipe to remember because it is a 1:1:1 ratio. This creates a cocktail that is equally boozy, bitter, and sweet. Once you try the original, I encourage you to experiment—add more Campari for a bitter bite, or reduce the amount of sweet vermouth and Campari to soften these flavors. If you've never tried Campari, or tried it once and weren't a fan, give it another shot. It's been said that after tasting it three times, only then will you love it.

750 ml bottle gin

750 ml bottle Campari

750 ml bottle sweet vermouth

16 oz water

Orange twist or slice, for garnish

Add gin, Campari, sweet vermouth, and water to beverage dispenser or pitcher. Chill until cold.

When ready to serve, prepare orange garnishes and set aside. Add one large ice cube to each glass. Stir chilled cocktail and pour into glasses.

Garnish each cocktail with an orange twist or slice.

NEGRONI SBAGLIATO

A sparkling spin on the Negroni that is lower in alcohol because the gin gets replaced with sparkling wine.

For one

1 oz Prosecco

1 oz Campari

1 oz sweet vermouth

Orange twist or slice, for garnish

For the batch

750 ml bottle Prosecco

750 ml bottle Campari

750 ml bottle sweet vermouth

16 oz water

Orange twist or slice, for garnish

Add the Prosecco just before serving to ensure it doesn't go flat.

THE GLENTOWER

This recipe comes from my dear friends, Scott and Shannon Austin. The Glentower—named after the street where they live and host fabulous gatherings—is their house cocktail. It's a spin on the classic Fitzgerald, a type of gin sour. I don't have enough room on this page to express how much the Austin Family means to me—we've shared life's best moments, worst tragedies, and many, many memorable cocktail parties. Even though we now live 2,000 miles apart, our lives are woven together in such a way that they will always be family.

FOR ONE

1 ¼ oz gin

1 oz St~Germain

1 oz lemon juice

¼ oz simple syrup (page 13)

1 dash (or less than ¼ tsp) absinthe

1 dash Angostura bitters

Lemon peel, for garnish

CITRUS JUICE
1 lemon = 1 ½ oz juice
14 lemons = 21 oz juice

Add ingredients to a shaker filled with ice. Shake for 20 seconds until very cold. Strain into a coupe glass. Twist lemon peel over cocktail, then garnish.

Batch
20 SERVINGS

78 oz | 9 ¾ c | 2 ½ qt

750 ml bottle gin

12 oz St~Germain

20 oz lemon juice

5 oz simple syrup (page 13)

14 oz water

½ oz absinthe

18 dashes Angostura bitters

Lemon peels, for garnish

Add ingredients (except bitters) to a pitcher and chill. Just before serving, add bitters to chilled cocktail, stir, and pour into coupe glasses. Twist a lemon peel over each cocktail, then garnish.

FRESH JUICE

Fresh squeezed grapefruit juice always tastes better. Try out different varieties, such as Ruby Red, Oroblanco, Pink, Pomelo, and Thompson.

In a pinch, check your local store for fresh-pressed, unpasteurized juice.

2 oz gin
½ oz St~Germain
2 ½ oz grapefruit juice
Grapefruit slice or peel, for garnish

Add gin, St~Germain, and grapefruit juice to a shaker filled with ice. Shake for about 20 seconds.

Strain the cocktail into a highball glass filled with cubed ice.

Garnish with a grapefruit slice or peel.

FRENCHIE

71 oz | 8 ¾ c | 2 ¼ qt

The Frenchie is as easy to drink as it is to mix up. The refreshing drink features St~Germain, a French liquor made from elderflower blossoms. If you like the Greyhound, give this one a try.

750 ml bottle gin

6 oz St~Germain

30 oz grapefruit juice

10 oz water

Grapefruit slices or peels, for garnish

Combine gin, St~Germain, grapefruit juice, and water in a pitcher. Chill until cold.

Prep the grapefruit garnish as desired. Cover with a damp cloth and set aside.

When ready to serve, fill highball glasses with cubed ice. Stir chilled cocktail then pour into glasses.

Garnish with grapefruit slices or peels.

CITRUS JUICE

4 grapefruit = 32 oz juice

RECIPE TIP

There are other brands of elderflower liquor available on the market. St~Germain is the original, and I like that it is naturally flavored. If you purchase another brand, you might need to adjust the volume to balance the flavor and sweetness.

RUM

PERFECT TOUCH

I originally created this cocktail for a live video tutorial on summertime drinks. My mom and aunt watched the episode, mixed up a batch, and called to tell me about the fun they were having together. In that moment I was reminded—the heart of my cocktail passion is about bringing people together. Perfect Touch is dedicated to sisters, to connecting over drinks, and enjoying small, meaningful moments in life.

FOR ONE

2 oz white rum

1 oz lime juice

1 oz basil simple syrup (page 15)

2 strawberries, remove stems and quarter

3 tablespoons blueberries

2 oz sparkling water

Strawberry & basil sprig, for garnish

Add blueberries, strawberries, lime juice, and basil simple syrup to a rocks glass and muddle together. Then add rum and fill glass with crushed ice. Top with sparkling water. Garnish with a strawberry and basil sprig.

Batch

12 SERVINGS

80 oz | 10 c | 2 ½ qt

750 ml bottle white rum

12 oz lime juice

10 oz basil simple syrup (page 15)

24 strawberries, remove stem and quarter

1 pint blueberries

12 oz sparkling water

Strawberries & basil sprigs, for garnish

Muddle berries in a punch bowl or pitcher. Add lime juice, basil simple syrup, and rum. Chill until cold. When ready to serve, top with sparkling water and stir. Ladle into glasses filled with crushed ice. Garnish with strawberries and basil sprigs.

INGREDIENT SWAP

You can substitute other seasonal fruit like raspberries and blackberries, or use mint simple syrup (page 17) for a fruity mojito.

CITRUS JUICE

12 limes = 12 oz juice

RECIPE TIP

This recipe is built in a serving glass so be sure to stir your cocktail before consuming to mix the ingredients and balance the flavors.

HEMINGWAY DAIQUIRI

This cocktail was created in Havana, Cuba, for Ernest Hemingway. The famous writer could often be found drinking with artists, authors, politicians, and actors. The recipe has taken on many variations since its creation, so I encourage you to play with the volume of each ingredient until you find your favorite version.

FOR ONE

2 oz white rum

¼ oz Luxardo Maraschino Liqueur

¾ oz fresh lime juice

½ oz fresh grapefruit juice

½ oz simple syrup (page 13)

Grapefruit peel, for garnish

Add ingredients to a shaker filled with ice. Shake for 20 seconds. Pour through a mesh strainer into a coupe glass. Remove a strip of grapefruit peel. Hold over glass, outer skin side down, and quickly squeeze to release essential oils. Garnish.

CLASSIC DAIQUIRI

Don't mistake this classic cocktail for the overly sweet, blended version with the same name.

2 oz white rum

1 oz fresh lime juice

¾ oz simple syrup (page 13)

CITRUS JUICE

9 limes = 9 oz juice

Batch

12 SERVINGS

59 oz | 7 ¼ c | 1 ¾ qt

750 ml bottle white rum

2 oz Luxardo Maraschino Liqueur

9 oz fresh lime juice

6 oz fresh grapefruit juice

5 oz simple syrup (page 13)

12 oz water

Grapefruit peels, for garnish

Remove a long piece of grapefruit peel for each drink. Cover with a damp cloth and set aside. Add rum, fruit juices, simple syrup, Luxardo, and water to a pitcher. Stir to combine, then chill. When ready to serve, stir chilled cocktail and pour into coupe glasses. To finish each drink, hold a peel, outer skin side down, over a glass and quickly squeeze to release essential oils. Garnish.

PAINKILLER

The Painkiller—a classic tiki cocktail—was invented sometime in the 1970s. It's similar to a Piña Colada but easier to make—no blender required—just quickly shake up a few tasty ingredients. Be sure to use the name-brand cream of coconut, Coco Lopez, which you'll find in most grocery stores. Then, sit back and enjoy your vacation in a glass.

FOR ONE

2 ½ oz dark rum

3 oz pineapple juice

1 oz orange juice

1 oz Coco Lopez

Dehydrated orange wheel, for garnish (page 19)

Mint sprig, for garnish

Nutmeg, freshly grated for garnish

Combine rum, fruit juices, and Coco Lopez in a shaker with ice. Shake for 20 seconds. Strain into a highball glass filled with crushed ice. Garnish with nutmeg, orange wheel, and mint sprig.

Batch

10 SERVINGS

83 oz | 10 ¼ c | 2 ½ qt

750 ml bottle dark rum

30 oz pineapple juice

10 oz orange juice

10 oz Coco Lopez

8 oz water

Dehydrated orange wheels, for garnish (page 19)

Mint sprigs, for garnish

Nutmeg, freshly grated for garnish

Add rum, fruit juices, Coco Lopez, and water to a pitcher. Whisk together, and chill until cold. When ready to serve, stir cocktail and pour into highball glasses filled with crushed ice. Garnish with nutmeg, orange wheels, and mint sprigs.

CITRUS JUICE

1 orange = 3 oz juice

4 oranges = 12 oz juice

RECIPE TIP

Coconut cream and fruit juices separate quickly, so be sure to stir your batch often as you serve it.

FRUIT JUICE

If you have the time and energy to juice a pineapple, you should do it—you'll have an incredibly tasty drink. But, bottled pineapple juice is one of my exceptions to the fresh-is-better rule. I like to keep a stock of mini cans in my fridge for when the cocktail mood strikes.

FRUIT JUICE

If you have the time and energy to juice a pineapple, you should do it—you'll have an incredibly tasty drink. But, bottled pineapple juice is one of my exceptions to the fresh-is-better rule. I like to keep a stock of mini cans in my fridge for when the cocktail mood strikes.

JUNGLE BIRD

This tiki staple was created in 1978 by Beverage Director, Jeffrey Ong, at the Kuala Lumpur Hilton. The cocktail name was inspired by the hotel's bar, Aviary.

2 oz dark rum

¾ oz Campari

2 oz pineapple juice

½ oz lime juice

½ oz simple syrup (page 13)

Mint sprig, for garnish

1 ½ oz dark rum

½ oz spiced rum

¾ oz Campari

2 oz pineapple juice

½ oz lime juice

½ oz strawberry simple syrup (page 13)

Mint sprig, for garnish

Add rum, fruit juices, strawberry simple syrup, and Campari to a shaker filled with ice.

Shake vigorously for about 20 seconds until very cold.

Strain into a tiki-style glass, filled with crushed ice. Garnish with a mint sprig.

SEABIRD

103 oz | 12 ¾ c | 3 ¼ qt

A couple of years ago I discovered a social media event called, "Tiki the Snow Away" created by Dani DeLuna of Home Bar Girl. Every January—when half the country is snowed-in and wishing for warm weather—home bartenders post their favorite tiki cocktails and riffs. The Seabird is my take on the famous tiki concoction, the Jungle Bird. The spiced rum adds a warmth to battle the dreary Seattle winter, and the strawberry simple syrup reminds me that summer is just around the corner…eventually.

750 ml bottle dark rum

8 oz spiced rum

12 oz Campari

32 oz pineapple juice

8 oz lime juice

8 oz strawberry simple syrup (page 13)

10 oz water

2 bunches of mint, for garnish

Add rum, fruit juices, strawberry simple syrup, Campari, and water to a beverage dispenser or punch bowl. Stir to combine and refrigerate until chilled.

When ready to serve, fill tiki-style glasses with crushed ice. Stir chilled cocktail and pour into glasses.

Garnish with mint sprigs (and colorful paper umbrellas if you're feeling extra festive.)

DOUBLE BATCH (40 SERVINGS)

You'll be fully stocked for your next tiki-inspired party or summertime gathering, just add Hawaiian shirts and a Pu Pu platter!

1.75 L dark rum

20 oz spiced rum

750 ml bottle Campari

80 oz pineapple juice

20 oz lime juice

20 oz strawberry simple syrup (page 13)

24 oz water

3-4 bunches of mint, for garnish

CITRUS JUICE

8 limes = 8 oz juice

20 limes = 20 oz juice

MOJITO

The Mojito was invented in Cuba but there's some debate over exactly who mixed up the first version. The ingredients were adjusted and perfected by many bartenders over the years, making this one of the most popular rum drinks.

FOR ONE

2 oz light rum

¾ oz lime juice

¾ oz mint simple syrup (page 17)

1 oz sparkling water

3 mint sprigs (for recipe and garnish)

Lime wheel, for garnish

Muddle two mint sprigs and simple syrup in a cocktail shaker. Add lime juice, rum, and ice. Shake until cold, then strain into a glass filled with crushed ice. Top with sparkling water. Garnish with a mint sprig and lime wheel.

Batch

12 SERVINGS

55 oz | 6 ¾ c | 1 ¾ qt

750 ml bottle light rum

9 oz lime juice

9 oz mint simple syrup (page 17)

12 oz sparkling water

32 mint sprigs (for recipe and garnish)

Lime wheels (from 2-3 limes), **for garnish**

Muddle about 20 mint sprigs with simple syrup in a large glass measuring cup. Add lime juice and stir. Strain out large pieces of mint as you pour it into a serving pitcher, then stir in rum. Chill until cold. When ready to serve, add sparkling water to the pitcher. Fill glasses with crushed ice and cocktail. Garnish with mint sprigs and lime wheels.

RECIPE TIP

I don't like getting a mouth full of mint with every sip of my drink, so I use mint simple syrup in the recipe, and strain out muddled mint before serving.

If you prefer the traditional method of building a Mojito—muddle mint with unflavored simple syrup in a serving glass, then top with the other ingredients.

CITRUS JUICE

9 limes = 9 oz juice

EASY TIGER

Get on island time with this easy-drinking tropical cocktail that's bursting with pineapple flavor. Pineapple rum and pineapple juice meets Luxardo Maraschino Liqueur for a tiki-style cocktail. Feel free to substitute dark rum in place of the pineapple rum if that's what you have on hand.

FOR ONE

1 oz Plantation Stiggins' Fancy Pineapple rum

¼ oz Luxardo Maraschino Liqueur

½ oz lime juice

1 oz pineapple juice

¼ oz simple syrup (page 13)

Lime wheel, for garnish

Add rum, fruit juices, Luxardo, and simple syrup to a shaker with ice. Shake well, about 20 seconds. Strain into a glass filled with cubed ice. Garnish with a lime wheel.

Batch

12 SERVINGS

57 oz | 7 c | 1 ¾ qt

750 ml bottle Plantation Stiggins' Fancy Pineapple rum

2 oz Luxardo Maraschino Liqueur

6 oz lime juice

12 oz pineapple juice

2 oz simple syrup (page 13)

10 oz water

Lime wheels (from 2-3 limes)**, for garnish**

Add rum, fruit juices, Luxardo, simple syrup, and water to a beverage dispenser or pitcher. Chill until cold. When ready to serve, stir cocktail and pour into glasses filled with cubed ice. Garnish with lime wheels.

MR. STIGGINS

65 oz | 8 c | 2 qt

I have a love affair with Plantation Stiggins' Fancy Pineapple Rum. When combined with blood orange, you get a tiki-inspired, winter daiquiri. The clove notes in the pineapple rum and the cinnamon syrup adds a warming spice to the traditional daiquiri format, and the lime juice lends the right amount of brightness.

750 ml bottle Plantation Stiggins' Fancy Pineapple rum

16 oz blood orange juice

8 oz lime juice

6 oz cinnamon simple syrup (page 17)

10 oz water

Dehydrated blood orange wheels, for garnish (page 19)

Mint sprigs, for garnish

Add rum, fruit juices, cinnamon simple syrup, and water to a pitcher or punch bowl. Stir to combine, then chill.

When ready to serve, stir chilled cocktail and pour into glasses.

Garnish with mint sprigs and blood orange wheels.

PRO TIP

Plantation Stiggins' Fancy Pineapple rum, also referred to as "pineapple rum" or "Stiggins' rum" is delightful when served neat or with one large ice cube.

CITRUS JUICE

8 blood oranges = 16 oz juice

8 limes = 8 oz juice

AGED EGGNOG *Batch*

My friend Ben Huff has been perfecting this eggnog recipe for years. When I asked him if I could include it in this book, I received a spreadsheet comparing the exact ingredients in other recipes and his modifications. I love how much thoughtful detail he put into crafting this rich seasonal drink. The eggnog needs time to age, so make it a few weeks ahead to serve at your holiday party, or bottle and gift it to your favorite people.

SPIRITS

Many people add rum to their store-bought eggnog, which is why it is included in this chapter. While this recipe calls for bourbon, brandy, and rum, feel free to use only one or two of these spirits.

4 oz dark rum

12 oz bourbon

8 oz brandy

12 eggs

1 ½ cups sugar

4 cups whole milk

2 cups whipping cream

Nutmeg, freshly grated for garnish

Pinch of salt, optional garnish

MAKE TWO WEEKS IN ADVANCE:

Beat the eggs with a hand-held mixer until smooth.

Slowly add the sugar until incorporated. Then, slowly add rum, bourbon, brandy, and milk until mixed.

Store in a glass container in the back of the refrigerator, making sure it's 45° F or colder. Don't open or mix the jar. Let it sit for at least two weeks, but preferably a couple of months to allow the booze to mellow.

WHEN READY TO SERVE:

Mix the eggnog with a hand-held mixer. In a separate bowl, whip the cream until soft peaks form. Then, gently fold the cream into the eggnog mixture.

Serve in chilled glasses. Garnish with freshly grated nutmeg and a pinch of salt.

WINE

RED WINE SANGRIA *Batch*

29 oz | 3 ½ c | 1 qt

4 SERVINGS

Sangria—a punch made with wine, fruit, and liqueurs—can range in flavor from super sweet to very dry depending on the proportion of these ingredients and additions like sugar or juice. Cafe Ba-Ba-Reeba in Chicago makes the best sangria I've ever tasted. If you get the chance, it's not to be missed. Until then, try this batch of subtly sweet wine punch.

RED WINE

When making sangria, choose inexpensive Spanish wine such as Tempranillo, Malbec, Rioja, and Garnacha.

RECIPE TIP

It's very important to make sangria a day in advance to allow it to become naturally sweetened by the fruit juices. If you sample it right away, it will taste harsh and boozy, so be patient and let the flavors develop overnight. If you're in a rush and must serve it right away, add a little simple syrup to taste.

BEVERAGE CONTAINER

The liquid volume of this recipe will be roughly 1 quart (which equals 29 ounces, or 3 ½ cups); you'll want to choose a slightly larger pitcher to accommodate all the fruit.

750 ml bottle red wine

½ cup Cointreau

½ cup brandy or cognac

1 green apple, medium diced

1 orange, sliced

4-8 oz sparkling water

MAKE ONE NIGHT IN ADVANCE:

Pour wine, Cointreau, brandy, and fruit into a pitcher and give it a good stir.

Cover with plastic wrap and refrigerate overnight.

WHEN READY TO SERVE:

Stir well. Add cubed ice and a few pieces of fruit to each wine glass. Fill with wine, then top with 1-2 ounces of sparkling water, to taste.

WHITE WINE SANGRIA *Batch*

29 oz | 3 ½ c | 1 qt

4 SERVINGS

While most people think of making sangria with red wine, white wine acts as the perfect companion for fruit and liqueur. The wine punch is naturally sweetened by the fruit, with no added sugar, giving it a light and crisp flavor.

WHITE WINE
When making this recipe, choose inexpensive white wines such as Torrontés, Pinot Grigio, Albariño, and Viognier.

CITRUS SWAP
Use any fruit that's in season—experiment with pear, fresh cherry, mango, and passion fruit. Always include at least one type of citrus fruit for the best flavor balance.

WINE SWAP
Rosé also makes great sangria. Try using St-Germain instead of Cointreau, and replace the lemon and/or lime with grapefruit.

BEVERAGE CONTAINER
The liquid volume of this recipe will be roughly 1 quart (which equals 29 ounces, or 3 ½ cups); you'll want to choose a slightly larger pitcher to accommodate all the fruit.

750 ml white wine

¼ cup brandy or cognac

¼ cup Cointreau

1 cup strawberries, sliced

1 peach, medium diced

1 lemon, sliced and quartered

1 lime, sliced and quartered

MAKE ONE NIGHT IN ADVANCE:
Pour wine, Cointreau, brandy, and fruit into a pitcher and give it a good stir.

Cover with plastic wrap and refrigerate overnight.

WHEN READY TO SERVE:
Stir well. Add cubed ice and a few pieces of fruit to each wine glass. Pour and serve.

Frosé—the adult slushy—is made with inexpensive rosé wine. This warm weather cocktail tastes like a sophisticated ICEE (or Slurpee, depending on which neighborhood convenient store you loitered around as a kid). You'll feel nostalgic with every sip.

ROSÉ WINE

When making Frosé, choose inexpensive rosé wines made with bold grapes, like Rioja, Garnacha, and Cabernet Sauvignon.

750 ml bottle rosé wine

3 ½ oz strawberry simple syrup (page 13)

2 oz lemon juice

1 cup ice

Lemon slices, for garnish

MAKE ONE NIGHT IN ADVANCE:

Pour bottle of rosé into ice cube trays and place in freezer overnight. (The rosé won't freeze solid.)

WHEN READY TO SERVE:

In a blender, add the rosé ice cubes, lemon juice, strawberry simple syrup, and ice. Blend until smooth. Divide the frosé between wine glasses, and garnish with lemon slices.

Bendy straws are optional!

APEROL SPRITZ

The Aperol Spritz, an Italian aperitif, has made a big comeback in the last couple of years thanks to Aperol's acquisition by Campari. Aperol is lower in alcohol than its more bitter cousin, Campari, making it a refreshing go-to for happy hour or brunch. Aperol is the star here, but this cocktail is only as good as the Prosecco you use, so be sure to purchase a bottle that you would be happy drinking on its own.

FOR ONE

3 oz Prosecco or sparkling wine

2 oz Aperol

1 oz sparkling water

Orange slice, for garnish

Add Prosecco and Aperol to a wine glass filled with cubed ice.

Top with sparkling water. Garnish with an orange slice.

Batch

8 SERVINGS

51 oz | 6 ¼ cups | 1 ½ quarts

750 ml bottle Prosecco or sparkling wine

16 oz Aperol

10 oz sparkling water

Orange slices, for garnish

Add Prosecco and Aperol to a pitcher. Chill until cold.

When ready to serve, fill glasses with cubed ice. Add sparkling water to pitcher and stir well.

Pour into glasses and garnish with orange slices.

RESOURCES

Amazon (amazon.com)
Cocktail books, metal straws, silicon ice cube trays, Honsen Y-peeler

Bar Products (barproducts.com)
Best value for shaker tins, jiggers, strainers, tiki mugs, wide assortment of bitters

CB2 (cb2.com)
Glassware

Cocktail Kingdom (cocktailkingdom.com)
Shaker tins, jiggers, strainers, dasher bottles

Chairish (chairish.com)
Bar carts, vintage glassware

Crate & Barrel (crateandbarrel.com)
Glassware, beverage dispensers, pitchers

Estate sales and second hand stores
Vintage glassware, punch bowls, serving trays

Hedley & Bennett (hedleyandbennett.com)
Handmade aprons in fun color combinations

Libbey (libbey.com)
Glassware

Mover & Shaker Co. (moverandshakerco.com)
Cocktail themed apparel, enamel pins, patches

Sonic Drive-In (sonicdrivein.com)
Crushed ice by the bag

Target (target.com)
Bar carts, beverage dispensers, pitchers

Trader Joes (traderjoes.com)
Candied lemon wheels and ginger, dried fruit

Twine (truebrands.com)
Wooden muddlers

Viski (truebrands.com)
Glassware, bar tools, cocktail picks

W&P (wandpdesign.com)
Brass pineapple shaker, metal straws, ice cube molds, The Bartender's Knife

West Elm (westelm.com)
Bar carts, glassware

Williams-Sonoma (williams-sonoma.com)
Glassware

World Market (worldmarket.com)
Cloth napkins, glassware, serving trays

BOOKS

The Bar Book: Elements of Cocktail Technique, by Jeffrey Morgenthaler, Chronicle Books, 2014

Bar Chef: Handcrafted Cocktails, by Christiaan Röllich, W. W. Norton & Company, 2019

Batched & Bottled: Cocktails to Make Ahead, by Max and Noel Venning, Quadrille Publishing, 2018

Batch Cocktails: Make-Ahead Drinks for Every Occasion, by Maggie Hoffman, Ten Speed Press, 2019

Cocktail Codex: Fundamentals, Formulas, Evolutions, by Alex Day , Nick Fauchald, and David Kaplan, Ten Speed Press, 2018

The Coupe: Celebrating Craft Cocktails and Vintage Collections, by Brian Hart Hoffman, Hoffman Media, 2016

Good Things to Drink with Mr Lyan and Friends, by Ryan Chetiyawardana, Frances Lincoln Adult, 2015

Julep: Southern Cocktails Refashioned, by Alba Huerta, and Marah Stets, , Lorena Jones Books, 2018

Tiki: Modern Tropical Cocktails, by Shannon Mustipher, Rizzoli, 2019

Smuggler's Cove: Exotic Cocktails, Rum, and the Cult of Tiki, by Martin Cate and Rebecca Cate, Ten Speed Press, 2016

Winter Drinks: 70 Essential Cold-Weather Cocktails, by the Editors of PUNCH, Ten Speed Press, 2018

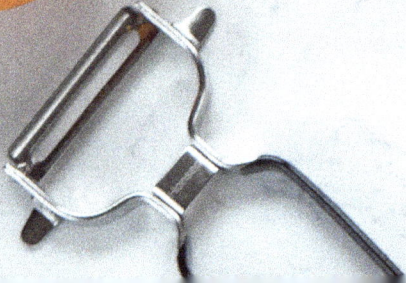

INDEX

KIM NEWTON ARISPE has appreciated the power of a good cocktail from an early age when she watched her grandparents gather with friends to sip margaritas and share stories. Years later, her passion for bringing people together over cocktails led her to create the website, Random Acts of Comfort, where she makes bar-quality beverages accessible to the home bartender. When she's not crafting cocktails for a party or a charity fundraiser, you'll find her on video teaching followers how to create seasonal drinks for easy entertaining. As a native Texan living in Seattle, she enjoys mixing up margaritas and hunting for good Tex-Mex with Bobby, her husband of 20 years.

www.ingramcontent.com/pod-product-compliance
Lightning Source LLC
Chambersburg PA
CBHW060756150426

42811CB00058B/1420